I0762071

THE APPLAUSE OF SCIENCE

≈

NATURE POEMS

Thomas Peter Bennett

Goose River Press
Waldoboro, Maine

Library of Congress Card Number: 2021931866

ISBN: 978-1-59713-232-9 Paperback
ISBN: 978-1-59713-233-6 Hardcover

First Printing, 2021

Published by
Goose River Press
3400 Friendship Road
Waldoboro ME 04572
e-mail: gooseriverpress@gmail.com
www.gooseriverpress.com

In the beauty of poems are the tuft
and final applause of science.

—Walt Whitman
Leaves of Grass, 1855

The Applause of Science is a poetry collection that explores nature in diverse environments through the lens of science. The poems pay homage to Walt Whitman, whose sage appreciation of the amity between poetry and science made him the first American poet to tackle boldly the problem of reconciling these two seemingly disparate fields. As a poet of the natural world, Whitman tried to understand nature as accurately and thoroughly as possible.

Leaves of Grass is Whitman's central work and one of the most important books in U.S. literary history. He envisioned this magnum opus in 1855 as a living, growing, organic being of its own, and Whitman himself oversaw six significantly different editions of the book during his lifetime. Each edition until 1892 had many similarities to its predecessor but contained substantial textual variations, from poems that were added or edited out to revisions of old poems, the shifting and recombination of existing ones, and differing layouts. However, Whitman's 1855 *applause of science*—his exclamations, *Hurrah for positive science! Long live exact demonstrations! and Smile O voluptuous coolbreathed earth!*—resonate throughout all six editions.

The Applause of Science consists of seven parts. The first is REDUCTIONISM, a set of poems on the molecular biology of nature and several scientific hypotheses on the topic. RAIN, the second part, analyzes water—the substance of all life— in its myriad forms and appearances. In FLORIDA RIVER, the role of water as habitat for Florida's plants and animals is examined. MAINE TIDES lyrically transports the reader to the coastal summer haunts of Maine, where creatures and habitats stand in sharp contrast to those described in part five, FLORIDA GULF COAST. Part six, BARTRAM'S TRAVEL, is inspired by the Floridian places and creatures which stimulated William Bartram's great nature work,

Travels, and the many people who followed in Bartram's footsteps seeking out the plants and animals he described. Written from my current residence in Maryland, ENVOI, the final part, includes poems based on the changing seasons. This collection reflects my belief that the arts and sciences inform our experience and appreciation in our unending exploration of nature.

—Thomas Peter Bennett, 2021

ACKNOWLEDGEMENTS

I am grateful to the editors and publishers who stimulated and sustained my writing of many poems collected here.

Their journals are *Perspectives in Biology and Medicine; POET-ALK; Red Owl; The Pegasus Review; The Café Review; Puckerbrush Review;* and Chebacco: *The Magazine of the Mount Desert Island Historical Society.* The anthologies are *Bay Area Poets Coalition Anthology 14; The Annual Anthology of the South Florida Poetry Institute; Cosmos Club Poets through the Years: An Anthology; and the annual Goose River Anthology.* Chapbooks include *A Celebration on the 200th Anniversary of Bartram's Travels, 1791; Tidemarks; Aquarius; Flight; At the Beach.* The poetry books are *Nature, As One Sees It* (2002); *The River Widens* (2005); *A Celebration of John and William Bartram: In Philadelphia and Florida* (1993, 2005); *Hike On: Poems from Mount Desert Island, Maine (2008); Encore Seasons* (2017); *and Florida Sketches: William Baldwin Follows Bartram's Tracks* (2019). The science book is *Florida Explored: The Philadelphia Connection in Bartram's Tracks* (2019).

My special thanks to Richard L. Landau for sparking my science–nature poetry muse in 1973 by publishing "Reductionism: 7 Lessons" in *Perspectives in Biology and Medicine,* and to Wanda Ritner and Charlotte Staub Thomas for illustrations and creative design for early chapbooks and several books. I greatly appreciate the efforts of Deborah J. Benner—editor of the *Goose River Anthology* as well as of Goose River Press in Waldoboro, Maine—for her guidance and creativity in several poetry publishing projects. And everlasting thanks go to those who mentored my learning and prepublication efforts, particularly Fritz Lipmann, Mary Oliver, Helen Cruickshank, and Michael Bugeja. My wife, Gudrun Dorothea

Bennett, has joined my exploration and provided photographs and conversations for memories and publications.

Walt Whitman's quotes are from his *Leaves of Grass* (Brooklyn, New York, 1855). Quotes italicized in Part 6, Bartram's Travels, are mostly from William Bartram's *Travels* (1791). In the poem "Florida Explored in Bartram's Tracks," quotes are from *The Correspondence of Thomas Carlyle and Ralph Waldo Emerson, 1834–72* (Boston: Houghton Mifflin and Co., 1883). William Baldwin's letter poems (dated) are from *Florida Sketches: William Baldwin Follows Bartram's Tracks* (2019) and *Reliquiae Baldwinianae* (Philadelphia: Kimber & Sharpless, 1843). Audubon's quotes are from his *Journals and Ornithological Biography*. John LeConte's are from *Proceedings of the Academy of Natural Sciences*. Joseph Beaver, *Walt Whitman – Poet of Science* (New York: Octagon Books, 1974).

TABLE OF CONTENTS

≈1≈
REDUCTIONISM

For every atom belongs to me as good
belongs to you.

■

Hurrah for positive science!
Long live exact demonstration!

—Walt Whitman
***Leaves of Grass*, 1855**

Reductionism: 7 Lessons

1. ATOMS
CHON
        all Life is.
P and S
        too.
K and Na
        the cell knows
Mg and Ca
        too.

2. MOLECULES
Acids many,
        fatty and amino.
Bases several,
        A, T, G, and C.
Sugars few,
        5 C and 6 C.
Water simple,
        H two O.

3. BONDS
Carbonyls to amino,
        peptide linked.
Phosphoryl to carbon,
        diester joined.
Carbons to oxygens,
        glycoside bonded
Exalt the hydrogen bridge.

4. ATP
The solar furnace,
        Life-giving energy.
Light converted,
        Lipmann bonds formed.
Metabolic dynamo,
        ~phosphate generated.
Water splits ATP,
        Life is moved.

5. Proteins
Twenty amino acids,
        peptide glued,
primary structures form.

Helically twisted,
        hydrogen bonded,
secondary structures form.

Super-coiled,
        groups interact,
tertiary structures form.

Now come together,
        mysteriously stuck
quaternary structures form.

6. DNA and RNA
Two basic types,
        many structures.
Four components
        similarly linked.
Watson and Crick
        double-helixed.

(continued)

Novel features,
        life interest.

7. DNA→RNA→PROTEIN
Flow information,
        the gene has spoken.
T direct A, G do C,
        all in vice versa.
Semi-conserve,
        growth at the fork,
while enzymes,
        snip, zip, and link.

Single strands
        that are transcribed
from words of DNA
        to language RNA
carry forth
        from helix double
message programs,
        Life to be.

Improbable events
        that always occur
the bases of Life
        translate:
three by three,
        three to one,
the code of Life
        moves on.

Forgot?

Where did I leave
        the copy of the poem
that I was working on
        before I started reading
about RbAp48 in *Science?*
        I can't remember!

The Cutting Edge

At the cutting edge
        you see the sheet lightning.
You know the thunder is there.
        You wait and count.
One thousand one, one thousand two …

Dynamin

I have read that
        another mechanochemical protein
has been identified recently:
        Dynamin.

Based on dynamics
        a motive force,
dynamo but not dynamite:
        Dynamin.

It mediates interactions,
        microtubules slide but
what biological function?

Microtubules

CELLS NEED THEM.
THEY PULL
C C
H H
R R
O O
M M
O O
S S
O O
M M
E E
S S
APART.

Spontaneous Generation

That living organisms
        come from nonliving matter
was a belief for centuries.

Frogs came from mud,
        maggots from rotten meat, and
microbes from soups and broths.

Pasteur contradicted the microbe notion.
        Redi, earlier, maggots from meat.
Only, frogs from mud is unchallenged.

Chaotic Stirring

In a tidal basin the
        plants and animals,
and elemental non-life,
        atoms and molecules,
the biotic and abiotic,
        attached, floating, swimming,
suspended or dissolved
        make a tidal random walk
with Lagrangian chaos in
        trajectories of water parcels.
nature's elaborate tide pool.

Metamorphic Dilemma

You need great restraint
        when you discover
your beautiful plants,
        in your butterfly garden, are
being leaf stripped by
        boorish cutworms, hornworms
and caterpillars.
        Yes,
much restraint
        indeed!

Biochemist Explains Autumn Colors

"What causes autumn colors?"
        he asked.
"Night's length, weather, and leaf pigments,"
        she replied and added,
"Chlorophyll gives leaves their green color.
Carotenoids create yellow, orange, gold, and tawny hues.
Anthocyanins fashion blends of red, purple, and blue,"
        concluding,
"Long, dry summers, pre-winter cold snaps give shades of
        brown."

Snake in a Tree?

A gauzy, molted snakeskin
        draped around a bare oak branch,
pinned to a squirrel's nest,
        fluttered in the wind.

I watched and wondered—
        Did a snake climb the oak?
Wrap and rub around the limbs,
        sluff off its aged skin?
Did squirrels attach it to their nest
        as an ominous flag for intruders?
Hypotheses, but what proof?
        Do snakes climb trees?

Young John James Audubon answered,
        "Yes, snakes climb trees,"
in what became a scientific controversy.

Audubon painted a portrait of mockingbirds
        defending their tree nest against a rattlesnake.
Naturalist George Ord called it artistic imagination:
        "Snakes do not climb trees!"
Audubon published, described more evidence,
        "... snakes ascend to their nests ...
suck the eggs or swallow the young ..."
        Ord said, "Nonsense, a woodsman's tale."
But ...
        Audubon's field findings
were confirmed by others:
        "Snakes do climb trees."

Make No Assumptions

But if you do,
        check them out,
one by one and
        two by two,
And ask,
        what don't I know,
that I don't know?

≈2≈
RAIN

Smile O voluptuous coolbreathed earth!
Earth of the slumbering and liquid trees!

—Walt Whitman
***Leaves of Grass*, 1855**

Water Forms

Drizzle, rain or mist?
Their feel, their sound, their smell
arouse the poet.
Their particle size, precipitation
stimulate the scientist.
And you, reader?

Rain, Rain...

Rain is water
        H_2O
60 to 90%
        weight of life.

Rain prickled
        my skin and
delighted
        my senses.

Foggy

On a December morning,
        a dark shape landed
on a pin oak's high limb.
        A hawk?

Its head rotated,
        its rigid tail line straightened.
The broad tip, a red blur, or a sun glint?
        Pale breast feathers, orange-tinged?
Streaked or a shadow?
        A red-tailed hawk, I guessed.

The fog closed in.
        I was left with many doubts.
The bird, a foggy memory.

Frosty Morning

Naked trees
        reveal roofs
glittering with ice crystals.

As the sun's rays glide
        over the shadowed slates,
the ice melts like a glacier in retreat,
        becoming sky-mirrored puddles.

Snow Flurries

Coming at noon,
        just as predicted.
Stark tree branches
        silently await winter's dusting.

Finches, juncos, and sparrows
        seek tangled twigs for shelter.
Squirrels scurry to bough crannies
        for nests, the warmth of dead leaves.

Rapt nuthatches,
        serene in snowflakes,
poke at balcony suet,
        as I enjoy the silent overture
of nature's winter opera.

After Midday Rain

Choruses of frogs,
        Rana, Bufo, Hyla,
replace the choirs
        of birds,
Mimus, Sialia, Turdus,
        heard at sunrise.

Crape Myrtle in Rain

When it rains,
        the crape myrtle
droops its
        ponderous breasts,
of rose petaled
        flowers.

Welcomed Rain

Burst and downpour,
        thunder and lightning,
wind and waves rising on
        the thirsty river.

Mangroves bend,
        grasses flatten,
palm fronds droop as
        earth soaks.

After weeks of
        August heat, and
a month of drought,
        a new cycle begins
with a tropical storm.

Past Present

After the rain,
        I flop in the
watery grass, roll over
        and wash away the sweat
of an afternoon digging
        for clay-encrusted fossils.

A flash brightens the
        leaden sky, followed by
a thunder cymbal, and
        a distant drum roll,
as when nimble creatures,
        now extinct, lolled in the grass
after the rain.

Lichen Repast

After the rain,
        the ground was garnished
and seasoned with morsels
        of leathery primitive plants.
A banquet for beetles and slugs.

Millipede Mystery

After the rain,
        millions of legs
tramp from leaf litter
        down to the pond.
Hours later, a multitude of
        death-coiled millipedes float
bloated on the pond surface.
        Was it the rain?

After the Rain

Is a wonderful
        time for mating
as every chartreuse
        tree frog knows.

Rain Drops

From my study window, I gaze
        as raindrops align, evenly spaced,
on the balcony rail
        and randomly drop
like life's happenings.

Afterward

The rain
last night
decorated
        trees with
        dazzling
        diamond
        drops
and
drooped
        their
        leaves.

Rain Pastoral

Late afternoon
          in summer,
it is greenish copper
          outdoors.
Tree trunks and atmosphere
          are copper,
all else is green—
          leaves, grass, and ferns.
The scene is still,
          just the rain smell,
          and the distant thunder.

≈3≈

FLORIDA RIVER

Flow on, river! flow with the flood-tide,
and ebb with the ebb-tide!

—Walt Whitman
Leaves of Grass, 1856, 1891

River Watch

1. Early
It's rained all night and
        I heard the a/c shift from
cool to heat an hour ago.

Dry, warm air wafts
        across my desk,
carryings a coffee aroma
        that alerts me.

Across the river,
        mangroves are illuminated
by the rising sun.

I look upward through the skylight,
        through fronds of sable palms, and
see an indigo sky patched
        with cumulous clouds.

A wood stork's silhouette
        soars upward in a draft.
A cold front is passing through.

2. Later
I follow the sun's
        silver glide across
the river until I reach
        the mangrove islands.

I loll in my kayak
        near the shady shore and
mangrove stilts.
        I splash pinkish water
and a little blue heron jump—flies.

The mangrove's prop roots
        are festooned with oysters.
Its branches support
        an egret's and a heron's
platform nests of twigs.

The cry, cry of the gulls
        overhead and
the increased tidal flow
        fill my mind.

I paddle upriver against
        outgoing tide currents,
across the river toward
        the dock and nest
of the kayak.

Tidal Change

The river estuary oscillates,
        fluctuates among
the mangrove islands
        and its shores,
driven by sun and moon,
        wind, and storm surges,
ebbs and flows, days, and nights.

1. Morning Low (0.6 feet, 5:30 a.m.)
Great blue heron struts,
        ankle deep,
across the emerging mud,
        as the sunrise glimmers
on wavelets, draws
        attention to pinfish
and marsh crabs..

2. Morning High (2.2 feet, 11:15 a.m.)
Mud flats and
        the dark waters
reflect the overcast sky.
        As waves curl
around the dock pilings,
        a great blue heron
perches and preens its
        shoulders, breast, and neck.
Marsh crabs,
        landside of the mangroves,
catch the bird's attention,
        and he floats down to feed.

3. Evening Low (-0.1 feet, 7:30 p.m.)
After the rain, the gray
        mirror water surface reflects
images of two great white
        egrets fishing the shallow flats
on both sides of the river.

4. Evening High (1.5 feet, 1:10 a.m.)
The dark waves are running,
        rushing away from the dock,
splashing mangrove stilt tops,
        as silver crests shimmer and
reflect the full moon.

Crab Man

You arrive daily,
        the sun your clock,
and abruptly stop your
        weathered skiff at each
orange buoy and
        quickly lift from
the river
        your galvanized crab traps.
The squirming crabs,
        you drop into
barrels of ice.

Fish and conchs, you
        toss overboard
for the pelicans,
        who splash for
lazy rewards.

Rain Encore

Gulls hang in the sky,
        over the river,
at sunset.

Palm fronds thrum
        moist gentle breezes for
a chorus of crickets.

Raindrops keep dropping
        from a dock's tin-roof as
a skiff rocks in its cradle.

Dawn and Dusk

1.
Mourning doves' long coos,
        hoot a plaintive end
to the owl's night.

Misty grayness lifts above the
        river as yellow
flashes of sunlight strike
        jumping mullet
that create
        slashes in the water.

2.
Full moon setting casts
        a sterling bridge across
the river.

A yellow-crowned night
        heron barks *quok, quok.*

A dewdrop slides down
        a mangrove leaf.

Mist outlines a sheet
        web spider's nest.

Dew-lined silk links
        mangrove prop roots
and yellow flowered branches.

(continued)

Marsh spider, upside-down,
    awaits a meal,
a mosquito, black fly, or midge.

Darkness

After dark,
        after the rain,
they align river side,
        and begin a grunting chorus.

They survey the
        river's expanse and
the miasma of fog
        over its shimmering surface.

Some dive into the
        dark unknown, searching
for water bugs and slugs.
        Those onshore continue
chorus croaking; cheering.

Ecolights

Miniature twinkles, flickers,
        random bursts at dusk,
among white and red mangroves.

Firefly luciferase,
        catalyst for luciferin,
illumines the river's edge.

Aquarian Celebration

Wow! Wow!
        Two in a row ...
A meteor shower
        radiating from Aquarius.

Earthly visible in
        the dome of the night,
framed by treetops,
        above a darkening river.

The Aquarids were
        brief flaming illuminations,
balls of fire in the sky ...
        giant frosted rain drops at night
from Aquarius.

View from the Dock

As I scan
    the afterglow,
a dolphin breaks
    the river's glassy skin.

An exuberant companion
    slashes the rose
water reflections.

Their fins' ripples merge
    into a colorful
river montage.

Lichen World

After the rainstorm
        the river path was littered
with twigs and branches,
        splotched with leathery,
yellow, gray, and brownish,
        primeval plant life—
a botanical wonderland

An Immature Preening

A yellow-crowned night heron
        hunches on the dock with
one yellowish-green leg folded
        under its breast.

Cocking its head,
        the heron starts to preen.

Its stocky bill fluffs
        beige breast feathers and
cleans a russet-specked neck,
        that stretches
for combing
        opened wing feathers.
The bill pulls off loose bits of
        down that fly in the breeze.

In an intermission,
        the heron lowers its upheld leg,
stretches and spears a marsh crab
        crawling on the dock.
Flips the crab and
        swallows it head-first.

Preening,
        trimming and cleaning,
continues, with pecking,
        around the thighs
and down each leg.

The heron massages its head,
        rubs its breast feathers,
kneads under its wings until
        head feathers stand on end.

Turning its head back around,
        the immature preens back feathers,
then returns to its one-legged stance.

Fishing Rights

Three snowy white egrets and
        a tricolored heron
sprint along the river shallows,
        squawking and flashing their wings
as three female mergansers cruise,
        submerging their sleek orange bills
under the water, below eye level,
        invading the territorial waters
of the egrets and heron.

Later, the three snowy sentinels
        at the water's edge
fly, flash, and land, to
        keep three cruising grebes at bay,
while the tricolored
        feeds nearby.

The discouraged grebes
        skim across the river and
swim underwater, but
        before they reach their
island destination, the
        snowies and tricolored
arrive at their feeding
        island, on that side of the
river and, again, become shore
        sentinels.

Alfresco

A turkey vulture perches
        on the dock, and
overlooks the
        low-tide mangrove muck
as her mate hovers, and lands
        where their fledgling brood
is scavenging.

One chick strips
        a catfish carcass
flesh from bone.
        Another picks away
at the soft meat within
        an open oyster.
        Another pecks the
shell of a blue crab
        stranded by the ebbing tide.

She-vulture flies down and
        joins them.

Great Egret

A large white bird
        landed on the dock.
In attack position…

Its beak, a yellow stiletto, with
        greenish-bronze streaks,
led to its beady laser eyes,
        yellow, with a black pupil
nestled in its white head.

The egret, tall with
        polished, jet-black legs,
stood and gazed at
        a container of
bait shrimp.

Night Hunter

A yellow-crowned night heron
        stalks the dock at sunset
for marsh crabs that
        scamper between decking gaps.

The gray-bluish bird,
        with a bold head pattern,
white cheeks, vermilion eyes,
        and long yellow legs
turns, as wind fluffs its
        yellow crown and waves
its white plume.

With no prey success,
        it floats down
to grassy shore flats
        and continues hunting.

The heron moves erectly with its
        neck extended,
yellow-topped head
        motionless,
red eyes focus on
        crab holes among grass tufts.

Heron lifts one foot,
        takes a ten-second stride.
Neck extends forward,
        bill poised,
its head
        rocks back and forth.
The dark, thick bill
        flash-strikes a dashing
crab and wedges it,
        in a vise grip.
The crab's armor crunches
        and, along with its flesh,
is sucked backward into
        the night heron's gullet.

Midnight Hoot

Barred owl calls,
        hoohoo-hoohoo,
        hoohoo-hoohooaw.
I call back eight hoots.

From the onyx sky,
        a moonbeam glints the river.
Barred owl cries eight hoots,
        and the water darkens.

A Warbler

Plucked a worm from
        the dew-dropped grass.

The warbler—
        one of fifty-four species
in seventeen genera of
        Western Hemisphere birds,
Peterson called "butterflies of ornithology"—
        was unknown to me.

As a peeping birder,
        I watched the warbler beating the
ground with the worm and then
        eating it in one swallow.

Great Blue Heron

The slate-blue bird
        surveys
the river shallows.

His golden eyes,
        with onyx pupils,
take advantage of
        the full stretch
of a serpentine neck.

A silent step,
        and the slender neck
changes to a tensioned,
        flattened S.

Head and bill shoot forward!

The bill rivets a baby
        stingray swimming in range.
Pierced in the head,
        the bat-like ray
swishes its tail.

The heron moves
        toward a mud flat,
where it drops,
        stabs, drops and stabs,
the ray ten times,
        then carries it
back to the shoal.

The heron swirls the ray
    in a wavelet,
and executes
    a decisive binding puncture,
then moves the ray
    to the rear of it bill
and gulps.

Tricolored Heron

1.
A slender, gray-blue heron with
        reddish neck and white belly
sounds guttural croaks and squawks.

Also called the "Louisiana heron," it
        is common in Florida and the Deep South,
but never in large numbers, and nearly always
        solitary.

As it searches for
        frogs or fish,
the tricolored
        moves gracefully,
feeding in deep water
        with its legs submerged.
It often appears to swim.

2.
The heron hunts at low tide,
        in the mud flat,
near the mangroves.
        It wades deeper and
sprints after darting, splashing fish.
        It raises its bluish gray wings and
extends white feathers that
        flow from its glossy head crest.

It makes a quick bill thrust
        into the water,
flips a pierced fish,
        and with a gulp
swallows it live.

The heron stalks
        through exposed
mangrove prop roots,
        tracking fish with
an alert red eye and poised beak

Zwarr-wharra-whraa-boom-boom!

A motorboat wake disturbs
        the heron's
shadowed stealth.
Wings stretch,
        its white back-patch rises,
bluish wing feathers flash upward.

3.
At sunset,
        forge rays intersect
tannin wavelets
        that ripple over muck flats,
strawberry chocolate.

A tricolored glides,
        drops at
the stingray-pitted edge.

Its focused beak
    traverses as it stalks.
Its mottled head and neck
    reflect in the dark waters.

The lone hunter,
    on a dainty walk,
strikes its bill
    into water,
snipping a fish,
    then quick swallows
river quenches.

Little Blue Heron

The slate-blue
        bird stands
in the shallows
        as its head scans
the shoal for fish.

Its black-tipped,
        bluish bill is
a short jab away from food.

A fast thrust impales
        a minnow.

The little blue makes a
        sliding step and the
reflections of the
        captor and its prey
are broken by ripples.

Titivating

On the river, a
preening loon
douses,
levitates,
flaps its wings,
flattens its feathers, and
oils its squeaky quills.

Ruby Red

The eye color
of five species
of loons,
glows,
and fires
loon legends
and superstitions.

Yellow Throat

A brilliant yellow
        patch creeps from
leaf into shadow,
        drops down to
a river rock—
        the petite bird with
a bold black mask,
        shining yellow throat,
a golden profile against
        roan granite—
witchity, witchity, witchity.

Osprey

After sunset,
        perched
on the high-tension line,
        surveys the river
as darkness transforms
        silver and pinks into
blackness.

A power dive,
        talons spread forward,
feet first,
        splash, swoosh.

With an impaled mullet
        in its talons, the osprey
zooms to flight speed,
        and cruises toward its
island nest.

Wood Stork

1. Bathing

In the river,
        its head submerged,
body soaked and
        wings splashing,

goes back to the flats
        where orange-pink feet
activated by dark legs
        scratch its head.

Wings spread,
        it struts around,
to air-dry its
        feathers.

2. Fishing

A foot deep
        in river shallows,
with its bill submerged,
        from the base of its beak,
and trap-opened
        about three inches,

Head down,
        the stork walks forward,
lifts its pink foot,
        extends its toes
with foot-stirring
        startles fish out of the weeds.

With the fastest reflex known,
        the stork's
submersed shabby bill
        snaps shut when
a fish swims into
        the open deadfall.
Instinctive force,
        and sharp-edged bill
prevent any escape.

The stork raises its flinthead,
        gives a quick backward head jerk
and swallows.

3. Nesting

On a mangrove island,
        they appear
from a distance as
        white paper debris
covering the green acre
        floating on the river,
tethered by brown, sinuous mangrove props.

4. Flying

Five feet above the river,
        flap, flap, flap, flap,
flap, flap, flap,
        glide, glide, glide, and glide.

The Catch

They line up along the river,
        on the flats,
each fishing,
        its own way.

1. Snowy Egret
Its golden slippers wiggle
        in the shallows.
The wavelets lap around
        its feet and legs as fish
dart for safe hiding.

The snowy's jet-black
        lance beak strikes
surface fish, flips them,
        and swallows.

2. Roseate Spoonbill
Reddish oval body,
        contouring into
a pink flecked neck and
        bare gray-green head
equipped with
        a spoon-shaped bill,
that moves in an arc
        around its body,
at eye depth,
        sucking up mud,
crustaceans and insects.

Punctuated by a spoonbill gasp,
        as if a burp out of water,
it continues vacuuming, munching.

3.White Ibis
Erect with
        its black wing tips,
hidden at rest, its
        red, bare face
leads.

A down-curved bill
        pierces the mud.
It seizes a crab, does
        a quick extraction,
a gulp and
        a swallow.

Spanish Moss

Between the last sliver
        of sunlight
and the dazzling
        blood moon,
a mysterious
        fragrance,
delicate and elusive,
        draws me
into a tangled grove
        of live oak trees …

Ancient sentinels decorated
        with bluish gray
flexuous tresses,
        bedecked with
tiny, fragile,
        cyan-colored flowers.

Like a night moth
        in a gentle forest breeze,
attracted by the
        fragrant essence,
I search for locks of moss
        and gather flowered
strands for musing.

Drummer

Hammering sounds
    came from the trees,
tap, tap, tap.
    I looked up.
saw beak on wood,
    beak on wood,
tapping, tap, tap.

A black body, white fringed,
    slung under a lifeless branch,
claws in place, gripping.

Beak to wood,
    a red-crested, black head darted
side to side,
    tapping, tap, tap, tap.
A piliated Krupa in the trees
    drumming, tap, tap, tap.

Traps

Fog at dawn reveals
        spiders' craft.

A dewy sheet web
        links grass blades
and girds weed stalks.

Tension-web filaments
        tether tree branches.

Filmy domes disperse
        reflected light from
sticky capturing webs.

Attending each web,
        a spider eagerly awaits
an insect meal.

Low Tide

1. Morning
The stingray glides
        over the murky bottom
near the dock.

Pinfish school nearby,
        and a blue crab
shuffles through the silt,
probing cracks and crevices.

The ray stalls in the mud,
        its undulating wings reverse
and sand swirls upward,
        creating ripples on the water.

Pitted mudflats, caverns
        abandoned by stingrays
and crab holes pock the muck,
        among rooting mangrove props.

Boat-tail grackles swarm
        from the red mangrove tangles,
flock upward and split
        into two flights.

One zooms over
        the quilted low tide pattern,
the other returns
        to the mangroves.

2. Evening

Plates of algae
        cover the river-flat bed where
oystershells are strewn
        with mangrove fruits.

In the shallows,
        minnows and reflections
of rose clouds at sunglow
        disperse as
slow water motion
        creates wavelets.

Nine wood storks
        break in and out
of flight formation.
        They glide,
flap wings and
        move in a
staggered V.

Two laggard juveniles
        with yellow bills
arrive five minutes later,
        trying to catch the flock.

Mullet—silver, blunt-headed fish
        with bulging eyes—
jump and splash at sunset.

Sunset

Flocks of boat-tail grackles
        fly from mangrove islands—
cross the river and descend upon
        oaks and high-tension wires.

Formations of wood storks and
        an occasional lone heron,
fly homing paths downriver.

A random mullet slashes the water,
        as pairs of little blue herons
glide on nesting missions.

Pink cirrus clouds develop,
        veiling a powder-blue sky.

The rose-colored sun
        becomes engulfed in
grayness and
        disappears on a
mangrove horizon.

The river runs pink
        and blue-gray.

River of Life

From the river's freshwater
        origins, through its estuarine
beginnings,
        it is a myriad of habitats—
homes for plants and animals
        that live in or near its waters.
Here they breed, nest, feed, and nurture
        life communities
that interact with the non-living world
        to form the river's ecosystem—home.

The Paleo-Indians,
        thirteen thousand years ago,
found this sanctuary
        as they established
camps along the river.

Native dwellings prevailed
        until the nineteenth century,
when the riverbanks
        were transformed by sugar cane
and cattle ranches.
        Commercial ventures and transport
brought other changes to the river—
        for resident algae, protozoa, shellfish, fin fish,
alligators, turtles, birds, and mammals.

The river's resiliency,
        living and non-living,
mitigates, over time,
        the increasing attacks
on the creatures and their
        unique homes on the widening river.

≈4≈

MAINE TIDES

The sniff of grass leaves and dry leaves,
and of the shores and darkcolored rocks.

—Walt Whitman
***Leaves of Grass*, 1855**

Tidemarks

From the cabin overlook,
        I meander along
the descending path to the bay.

From a rocky ledge,
        a hundred yards beyond,
the bay explodes in size.

Framed by glacial ridges,
        it extends toward
an endless sky.

Stunted junipers border
        the arid moss and fungus-
covered rock path.
        It leads to a chasm,
a broad geologic pit carved
        by glacial time, sculpted by waves.

Unmoved for centuries
        in an interlocking embrace are
weathered granite, a chaos of rocks.
        They mark the rise, fall, high, and low tides,
measure life's movement and evolution.

From the bay womb, to land's challenges,
        creatures advance on the tides.
Under control of sun and moon,
        bay water empties and fills the abyss.
The recessed tide reveals rocks encrusted
        with yellow and orange fungi.

Tide pools are glacial scoops
        of mirror-surfaced, hydro-connected crevices
—cracks, hollows, hidey-holes, niches, and notches—
        shelters for defenseless life.
Wavelets are food conveyer currents
        for filter feeders
barnacles, mussels, and worms.

Mollusk grazers trim, bite, smooth
        rock surfaces of algae,
lettuce, weed, grass, and kelp.

The scavengers
        —crabs, sculpins, stars—
live on the dead and dying.

Further down, toward the bay,
        lower tide pebbles
are a carpeted patchwork.

Once floating,
        swimming algae masses,
now pebble dry-docked
        await tidal resurrection.
Beyond, the bay is calm and reflects the sky.

Tidal Revelations

Full moon insures
        low spring tide,
uncovers the richness of
        intertidal life, habitats.

Bands of creatures—
        barnacles, then seaweed,
mussels and limpets—
        mark the tide's retreat,
while coral, seaweed, and
        whelks cling to shore rocks,
awaiting the tide's return.

A Miniature World

Appeared before me
        in craggy crevices
at spring low tide,
        a microcosm populated
by a myriad of creatures:
        algae, chitons, and stars.

The minute infinite,
        a secret world
whose small compass
        astonishes the eyes.
Tide pool busyness
        is like Manhattan
at mid-day.

The Chiton

A sluggish creature.

Creeps
along rocks
on one broad foot.

Carries
eight backpacks.

Between Tides

Lofty wave-splashed rocks at
        high tide,
dry uncovered pebbles at
        low tide,
mark bounds of life zones.

Between marks,
        microbes, plants, and animals
inhabit ageless haunts,
        nurtured by ebb and flow
between tides.

Limpets

Live the high life
        at night's tide
and graze on lofty
        algae-covered rocks.

At day's low tide,
        they descend
to resting sites,
        and sleep off
their high tide flings.

Barnacles

On water-splashed rocks,
        wait for food to wash past.
Hinged plates,
        hermetically closed,
when exposed at low tide,
        open at wave splashes.

Tiny casting nets,
        feathery barbed legs,
capture plankton,
        absorb oxygen.
Sated by the meal,
        the barnacle closes
its protective plates.

Marine Algae

In low tide, dry areas
        red, green, and brown algae
plaster rocks, pebbles
        of the intertidal zone,
crinkle and crack.

In life-teeming tidal pools
        they are lush scenery,
miniature forests,
        as full of creatures
as those of Amazonia.

High tide brings water
        to the drying algae—
a sure and certain
        source of resurrection.

Snail's Feast

Snail emerges
        through shell's trapdoor.
Its sluggish slimy body
        carries the black turban
while its head dines and shines
        the rock surface clean
of microscopic
        algae salad.

Mimicry

Superb actors!
Hermit crabs
Masquerade,
in abandoned shell homes,
as murex, turbans,
periwinkles, and unicorns.

Clingfish

Tadpole-shape when
        viewed from the top,
fish-like from the side,
        cling upside-down
to rocks, then
        swim away
to capture prey—
        microscopic crustaceans.

Polychaetes — Tube Worms

Many, varied,
        segmented worms,
burrowers, crawlers,
        tube-builders, swimmers,
a miniature, white-handled
        feather duster,
a microscopic garden hose
        squirting roses.

Aggregated Anemone

Have a name
        that says it all:
Anthopleura elegantissima.

The olive-green, vulva body
        is tipped with pink tentacles.
Elegantissima!

Mussels

Camouflaged,
        bluish-black nodes
attached to rocks
        by a DuPont-like process.

Soft creature,
        inside the double shell,
secretes a viscous liquid
        that hardens in seawater
to form fibrous
        linkage threads
called Byssus.

Elements of the Bay

A buoy is caressed
        by blue, drab water
of uplifting currents.

Changes, bobs ...
        changing directions
with the wind.

Changes, hue ...
        changing reflections
with the light.

Changes, shadows
        as clouds disperse
sunburst colors.

Silver ripples at midday
        golden ripples at sunset
fondle the buoy.

Bladder Kelp

Create brown islands in the bay.

Long stems,
        with bay depth's roots,
lead to flat bladed leaves and
        bulbous floats—
a home for harbor seals,
        an oasis for traveling gulls.

Naked Sex

She-crab
disrobes while mating.

Male crab carries
female in close embrace
until she loses her chitin clothing.

Out of her shell,
they mate in a silty frenzy,
and he lingers until
her new shell hardens.

Feeding Frenzy

Kaaw, kaaw, kaaw …
        raucous cries, *kaaw, kaaw …*

Flocking gulls
        group, gyrate,
water-glide, swim,
        in a seal's wake, with
herring in the lead.

Seal slices the water,
        dives, and creates a fishy
flotsam-jetsam allure
        for the boisterous gulls,
who hover, thrash wings
        and hungrily
kaaw, kaaw, kaaw, kaaw …

Partners

A gull circled,
    as fog veiled,
the bay.

A seal
    breached
the surf-fog border,
    glanced about,
curved its supple
    body above water,
then submerged.

The gull glided,
    settled, bobbed
and awaited
    fish scraps.

Working Low Tide

Herring gulls ride low tide,
        wings folded above water line,
bodies form a natural bay vessel,
        tails are wind rudders.

They nibble at crustaceans
        in floating rockweed, and
prepare for flight and hunt—
        pause to preen.

Dip their heads, splash
        with up-spread wings,
dunk their ivory breasts, and
        douse water under back feathers.

Into flight, they glide
        one hovers forward, then
backward, above the shallows,
        scanning the tidal pools.

A dive.
        A catch!

Soars upward,
        trophy in beak,
then releases—
        a free-fall clam, that
shatters on the stones.

Surveys, pauses,
          descends,
drop-lands,
          picks away
at its meal.

Star Hunter

A gull cruised the
low tide shallows,
spot-dipping its head
in boreal blue water.

It quick-dived, and
re-surfaced, dangling
a sea star in its red-
spotted yellow beak.

Clutching its squirming
victim, the gull paddled
to shore, threw the
creature forcefully
upon the rocky surface,
repeatedly stabbing the
bull's-eye, soft underside
orifice of the squirmer.

With each stab, the gull
pecked off a morsel,
swallowed, and centered
its prey on the cutting rock.

One webbed foot gripped
the star, while the beak
ripped off a piece of
one arm, and then another.

Bite-size remains were
    swooshed into the gull's
waiting beak, followed by
    a sip of bay water.

≈5≈

FLORIDA GULF COAST

The strata of colored clouds . . . the long bar of
maroontint away solitary by
Itself . . . . the spread of purity it lies
motionless in,
The horizon's edge, the flying seacrow, the fra-
grance of saltmarsh and shoremud;

—Walt Whitman

***Leaves of Grass*, 1855**

Gulf Shore Flight

I relax in a
        Delta Medallion upgrade
bulkhead, 1D window seat.

Atlanta to Sarasota is
        a fast-forward video of
a complex changing groundscape
        that I often snailed by car.

Rolling plains, thoroughbred rambles,
        lakes, meandering rivers, and streams
are connected to an undulating gulf.
        Primitive Florida.

The gulf side of peninsular Florida is
        barren, tropical, pristine, until
passing the north central zone, when
        Tarpon Springs and Tampa come into view.
I hold my native-born breath, glance
        at the landscape transformation
that continues until touchdown in Sarasota.
        Developed Florida.

Primitive Florida. Developed Florida.
        Florida, a paradox of change.

Gulf Water

Sand Beaches,
        canary-colored,
melt into blue water,
        creating
green gulf water.

My glance at
        gulf horizon
converges at
        the point
where
        green gulf water
and
        azure gulf sky
merge.

Waves of Grain

America's sea oats
          are its primal
amber waves.

Australian Pines

Your presence
          at beach edge
lends elegance
          to mystic
barren dunes.

Light shimmers on
          your gray-green
needles and
          reveals an
azure blue sky
          cut by an
osprey's silhouette.

Beach Morning

If you had been with me
    on Sanibel Beach,
You would have seen what I saw,
leaving your footprints
next to mine.

Tide marks
    evoked the past.
Coconut palms framed an alley
    between sea oats,
and tangled sea grapes.

In wet-packed sand
    crab carapaces marked
an earlier high tide
    leaving behind
driftwood, brown corpses—
    pen shells, sponges, crabs.

Off-shore,
    terns soared, glided,
stalled in mid-air,
    wings back,
air-to-water missiles—
    fish targeted.

I came to the cut.
        Flags flew against
a sapphire horizon.
        Fishermen on
jetty rocks held green nets.
        Casting, hanging on, reeling in—
hopping from foot to foot,
        anticipating the day's catch.

Further along, I saw
        a beach resident,
sun-dyed, with a screened rack hoe.
        She wore city sunglasses,
a lace-sleeved chemise, and
        surf mules.
Like a potato farmer
        she entered the surf-rows
and hoed beneath the waves.

She brought her harvest
        to the beach,
spread it on a linoleum sheet,
        culled the shell mass.
The keeps went into a bucket,
        throwaways recycled in the gulf.

The sun was high
        midway through the sky.
The wind and waves had tossed a
        sun-bleached tree on a dune plateau.
I rested there at noon,
        sky watching...

A brown pelican soared
        above the wave caps,
banked in a climbing turn,
        stalled in flight,
closed chute drops,
        flipping on impact.
Pelican mouth, fish-catch pouch
        captured stunned prey.
A sea gull floated nearby …
        as a dinner pet
to catch pelican throwaways.

An extended ibis family,
        in their white dress,
waded by, each dipping
        a brilliant red, long, curved
bill into wavelet shallows.
        Their ceramic blue eyes
scanned the beach scene.

Sun-bathed gulls
        swooped and
joined feeding pelicans.

A boat with three men
        cruised across the gulf horizon.
The first man, gray, tousled hair,
        was high placed, spotting.
The second, still a young boy,
        cruised while
the third, a bow man,
        older than the two,
posed with cast net
        in hand and mouth,
alert, contemplating …

I continued my walk…

Multicolored glass fragments
        lined the beach.
Gentle waves tumbled
        more onto the sand.

I thought, as I walked—

If you had been with me
        on Sanibel Beach
you would have seen what I saw
        and left your footprints next to mine.

Carr's Turtles

I think of Archie
  as I walk the white sand beach
where red flags outline
  real estate plots
with a sign posted:
  DO NOT DISTURB
  SEA TURLE NEST

Brown Pelican

As currents caress
        your white feathered keel,
you float in the waves,
        like an anchored tanker,
like a fixed buoy.
        Pelican, brown pelican,
what is your fixed anchor?

Beach Refugees

Each high-tide wave brings
        immigrant shells—
augers, miters, and mussels—
        to the white sand beach.

Their passage boats are
        pen shells, seaweed,
driftwood, and sponges.

Beach to Beach

Carrier, Tibia shells
        Moon, coral snails—
Where did you come from?
        How long your voyage?
You have explored many beaches!
        How many yet to come?

Gulf explorers in
        a sliver of
driftwood.
        Shells embedded in crevices,
on nature's ancient galleon,
        awaiting high tide to
carry them to other beaches.

Close nd Focused

When I
        dropped to my knees,
my eyes captured
        a myriad of miniature shells
Murex, Miters, and Frog.

I would
        show you,
if you would
        stop stooping
and sit beside me.

Coquina

Live in large colonies
on pristine beaches,
in the surf zone.

Short, fat rear end with
        long, tapered front.

Muscular head-foot
        burrows an inch deep
into moist sand.

Two rear-end siphons
        stretch to the surface,
for vacuuming algae and
        sweeping sandy grains
sparkling clean.

Shells hinged,
        even in death, a
ligament binds
        shell pair,
butterfly shells.

World of Donax

My toes burrow
        in the wet sand.
The wave foam recedes
        from the yellowish beach
exposing myriads of
        Coquina, Pompano shells,

Exquisitely varicolored,
        snow white to peach, rose,
lavender, and mauve,
        each shell etched with
ebony rays or a plaid pattern—
        Donax variablis Say.

As they burrow into
        the wet malted sand,
my toes and feet
        help them.

Hermit's Hideaway

Hermit's Hideaway Beach
        is a hundred yards long.
Every square foot
        is covered with shell condos—
conchs, bonnets, whelks,
        spindles, cones, janthinas—
each occupied by
        a satisfied
hermit crab,
        just the right size.

Transfiguration

Wedge-shaped shells
        of live coquinas
transformed after death
        by tide and time,
sand and surf,
        into
butterfly shells.

Funerary Treasures

Shellfish alive,
        with shell and soft body.
Shell remains after death,
        soft body becomes elemental.

Soft bodies entombed
        in gulf waters—
mythic souls in a
        funerary procession of waves.
Shells cast on distant beaches
        transfigured by sun—
resurrected by beachcombers as
        museum treasures.

≈6≈

BARTRAM'S TRAVELS

I hear the bravuras of birds.

—Walt Whitman

***Leaves of Grass*, 1855**

Florida

Mysterious, exotic Florida ...
        from earliest reports
in geological and climatic time,
        mastodons, rhinos, saber cats,
12,000-year-old human relics,
        to the Native peoples' first encounters
in 1513 when the Spanish arrived.

Spain ruled La Florida until 1763,
        when Spanish Florida became
Great Britain's fourteenth and fifteenth colonies,
        East and West Florida.

In 1765, King George III
        appointed John Bartram –
Philadelphian, plantsman, and botanist –
        as royal botanist
for the British Floridas.

Bartram's mission was to explore,
        beginning with the East Florida colony,
and document the Floridas' natural resources.

The Bartrams Explore Florida

In 1765–1766,
John Bartram and his son William,
a talented artist and field assistant,
explored upper, northeast Florida
and the St. John's River.

William returned in 1773
to explore both East and West Florida.

Florida continued as two British colonies
throughout the American Revolution,
and in accordance with the treaties ending the conflict,
East and West Florida again became
Spanish holdings in 1783.
Florida's Second Spanish Period began.

William Bartram returned
to his father's garden
in Philadelphia in 1777
and wrote his classic
TRAVELS,
THROUGH
NORTH AND SOUTH CAROLINA,
GEORGIA,
EAST AND WEST FLORIDA ...,
published in 1791 in Philadelphia.

William Bartram's Tracks

Do you know Bartram's Travels?
        Carlyle asked.
In classic coy correspondence
        with Emerson, he wrote:
Treats of Florida chiefly
has a wondrous kind
of floundering eloquence in it
and has grown
immeasurably old.

Carlyle's next proclamation –
All American libraries
ought to provide themselves
with that kind of book
and keep it as
a future biblical article –
        prompted others to seek
Bartram's ancient
        and future testament
and follow
        in Bartram's tracks,
as did
        Baldwin in 1813–1817,
Say, Ord, Peale, and Maclure in 1817–1818,
        Audubon in 1831 …
many others … and me.

Travels

(1791, First Printing)

I cautiously held the hand-sized book
        the cherubic Academy librarian solemnly gave me,
explored its binding, replaced in the nineteenth century,
        and opened it to the frontispiece, a portrait
of *Mico Chlucco the Long Warior or King of the Siminoles.*

Opposite, the title page in venerable detail:
        TRAVELS Through North & South Carolina,
Georgia, East & West Florida,
and in smaller type,
        The *Cherokee Country, The Extensive Territories ...*
Containing ... An Account ... BY WILLIAM BARTRAM.

At the top of the stained page, in script,
        the book's proud owner's India-ink notice:
Alexander Wilson's Book, Philad, Dec.9th. 1806.
        Wilson, befriended and impassioned by Bartram,
became the father-artist-poet of American ornithology.

The imprint of Mico Chlucco had bled
        in a brownish wash,
        caused by leaching of chemicals
into the paper fabric, onto touching pages,
Printed by James & Johnson. MDCCXCI.
This brown age I saw throughout the book.

Bartram's Observations Questioned

Many readers were eager to confirm Bartram's
exotic accounts of Florida's
plants, birds, snakes, alligators, and other creatures.
Whether they were fact or fantasy
was often the question
botanists and zoologists asked.

Some explorers became armchair travelers,
readers seeking specimens and information
from those explorers who trekked in Bartram's tracks,
using *Travels* as their guidebook and map.
Many followed in Bartram's tracks.

William Baldwin in Bartram's Tracks
Coastal Exploration
March 30, 1817

From Prospect Hill,
        on Fort George Island,
Baldwin wrote to William Darlington ...

Seated alone on the summit
        of the highest land on the island,
elevated about 50 feet
        above the surrounding country,
commanding an extensive
        and varied prospect of the ocean,
the mouth of the St. John's
        and the various hammocks
and cultivated fields.

There is then,
        within a circumference
of about 20 yards,
        all to be recognized
from my seat:
        Magnolia grandiflora, Querercus virens,
Laurus borbonia, Olea americana and Ilex opaca.

But among all these,
        not one flower is to be seen,
and the only specimen of flowers
        that I have in my portfolio,
after a ramble of two or three hours,
        is *Hopea tinctoria (Symplocos, Wild).*

But think not that there are no flowers
    to be found on the island.
Although the season is
    at least a month behind,
there are *Cnicus horridulus,*
    a few specimens of which would fill a cart;
Scorzonera pinnatifida, Krigia virginica, Houstonia;
    and the following, which may be new:
Galium, with very large hispid fruit.

One beautiful little *Lacerta bullaris,*
    the green lizard of Jamaica,
has made its appearance since I began to write.

Like the chameleon,
    this innocent little creature has
the faculty of changing color.

Could I only see a huge, "Magnanimous"
    (BARTRAM) rattlesnake,
it would help out
    my story very much.

During the five years I have been
    in this southern country,
I have seen but one living rattlesnake!

But had not BARTRAM been here before me,
    I would astonish you with my account
of the alligators.

I should like to wind up this
    interesting botanical letter
with some notice of insects
    could I call them by names less vulgar
than sand-flies, horse-flies, &c.,
    which have been buzzing about
me since I began to write.

I must now rise and "advance backwards"
    to Talbot Island.

Florida Landscape

April 19, 1817

That kind of land
        that is here called *hammocks*
is generally
        covered with live oak.

It is a little elevated
        limestone,
still abounding
        all along the coast
with undecomposed
        oyster shells, &c.

But by far
        the greatest quantity
of land along the seaboard
        is low pine barren
covered with *Pinus palustris*
        (long-leaf pine) principally.

Undergrowth is
        saw palmetto
with some fine shrubs,
        Andromedas, Bejaria, &c.

What we call savannas
        in this country
correspond pretty well
        with the prairies of the West.
But, *savannas* are seldom so extensive.
        The soil in them
is clayey,
        while the *pine barren* is sandy.

These are the most sterile
        of all descriptions of land.

Sandy Plains and Swampy Solitudes

Fernandina, December 6, 1816

Although the mere man
        of business or of pleasure
may see little to interest or amuse
        in the sandy plains
and the swampy solitudes
        of Georgia and Florida,
with the lover of botany,
        the case is far different.

He reflects that all-bountiful nature
        has clothed even the most sterile wastes
with some of her choicest ornamental,
        as well as useful, productions.

Who can behold
        the singular and beautiful
Befaria, or fly-catcher,
        without being charmed
by its splendor and fragrance
        or astonished at the faculty
it possesses of decoying insects!

The corolla of this plant
        secretes a tenacious substance,
which effectually retains flies
        and all other insects that alight upon it
until they perish:
        hence the name of flycatcher.

St. Augustine

Historian Michael Gannon commented,
"The first Thanksgiving was
celebrated in St Augustine, 1565.
St Augustine was up for urban renewal
when the Pilgrims arrived in Plymouth, 1620."

Royal Botanist John Bartram wrote in 1765,
"November 22 this morning early
As well as last night
Thundered at A distance W. N. W but
About sunrise y[e] day was Showery
Therm 67 we set out for Augustine
Billy walked & I rode on A hired horse."

On May 3, 1817,
Botanist-physician William Baldwin
Wrote:
"St. Augustine may be justly
considered to be
one of the healthiest
cities in the world.
Neither intermitting
nor remitting fevers
are known here,
nor have I heard
of a case
of pulmonary consumption."

Ornithologist John James Audubon wrote,
"St Augustine East Florida 23rd Novr 1831
The streets about 10 feet wide and deeply sanded
An old Spanish Castle once the Pride of this Peninsula
but now decaying fast
It is built of *Shell Stone* ... curious to the Geologist."
And he noted that nearby,
"We went on St Anastasia's Island and
collected some hundreds of shells
Saw great numbers of Water Fowls, Pelicans &c
Have shot only 2 birds to draw
One a beautiful Heron, the other a Sandpiper."

Audubon indicted St Augustine as the
"Poorest hole in the Creation ...
The Country around nothing but bare sand
hills—hot one day cold another etc etc
Sands, poor pine forests, and impenetrable
thickets of cactus and palmettos form the undergrowth."

He engrossed Lucy with a premonition:
"I am engaged in an arduous
undertaking but if I live to complete it,
I will offer to my country a beautiful monument of the
varied splendor of American nature, and of my devotion
to American ornithology."

Puc Puggy

In 1774, Chief Cowkeeper
        and the young men and maidens
welcomed William Bartram
        to Cuscowilla (now Micanopy),
in the Great Alachua Savannah.

They shook arms, not hands.
        Cowkeeper said, "You are come."

The pipe was filled and handed around
        followed by "thin drink."

Bartram explained his travels and mission
        of plant collection, and Cowkeeper
saluted, pledged support, and named Bartram
        Puc Puggy, or "Flower Hunter."

On Bartram's Alachua Trail by Car

Two Birthdays
On my birthday I treated myself
        and did something I have often wanted to do
but have not because of X, Y, or Z.

With the 200th birthday of *Travels* on my mind
The attention of a traveller,
        as he said,
should be particularly turned to Nature.

Wondering whether his visions
were still pristine romantic landscape scenes
or desecrated pollution sites, ecologically dead,

with map and a paperback version of *Travels,*
        I left on my birth morning in a sunroof Subaru
to celebrate Bartram in Alachua County.

River of Styx, River Styx
I stopped on the roadside and walked
        to a tributary creek, the River Styx,
and stood on the 1930s bridge.

Bartram's voice from creek-water perspective:
        a vasty extensive and sedgy marsh,
expanding Southerly like an open fan,
        seemingly as boundless as the great ocean.
Bartram's vision was little changed.

Lake Cuscowilla, Now Tuscawilla
As I drove the back roads I did not see
any gopher tortoises, as Bartram had on foot.
On SR 25A I halted on the grassy sideway
and walked to a fence, with my view,
like his,
obstructed by the vast forests upon the coast
of the great and beautiful lake of Cuscowilla,
its name now changed, and drought reduced
at no great distance from us, his vision intact.

Cuscowilla, Now Micanopy
SR 25A converges with 234 in Micanopy,
named for a later Seminole chief,
and like Bartram,
by *riding a mile farther,*
I too *arrived at Cuscowilla near the banks*:
a pretty brook of water ran through town,
and entered the lake just by.

Like Bartram's arrival among mythical Yamasees
mine was among *Doc Hollywood* myth producers.

Alachua Savanna, Now Payne's Prairie
On US 441, on the borders of the great
Alachua Savanna, now called Payne's Prairie,
I drove, as Bartram had walked,
for *near a mile,*
when at once opens to view,
the most sudden transition

from darkness to light,
that can possibly
be exhibited in a natural landscape.
Bartram's earlier vision was altered only
by automobiles traveling at highway speed.

I drove on, with sideway glance,
and like Bartram
surveyed *the extensive Alachua Savanna,*
a level, green plain, and scarcely a tree or bush
encircled with high sloping hills,
covered with waving forests.
Power poles and a four-lane highway
had changed the scene from a pastoral
Bartram vision to a futurist impression.

I turned and entered the Prairie Preserve
and could scarcely believe what I saw:
a bounding roe ...
just as in Bartram's account.
He views rapid approaches, rises up, lifts aloft

his antlered head, erects the white flag
and fetching a shrill whistle, says to his fleet,
"follow"; he bounds off. They knew their safety here.
A Bartram vision unchanged.

At the observation tower in the Preserve,
I was a surprised and delighted traveler,
just as Bartram had noted,
but being placed so near the great savanna,

how is the mind agitated and bewildered,
at being thus, as it were, placed on the borders
of a new world! The mind seems suspended
and impressed with awe.
I too was spellbound!

Back on US 441, I stopped at a Bartram-marked
observation ramp, walked out,
and a furrowing gator, Bartram's *old champion,*
perhaps absolute sovereign,
darts forth from the reedy coverts
on the surface of the waters;
at first as rapid as lightning.
Beer cans, fast food cups and straws glittered.

Great Sink, Now Alachua Sink
A side-trip brought me to Bartram's
long projecting point of the high forests,
beyond which opened to view a little creek,
meandering through the turfy plain,
joining the main creek that at length delivers
the water into the Great Sink.
On the savanna border, I saw the Alachua Sink,
exactly as Bartram had described it.

Like him, I descended the hill
onto a charming green meadow,
explored the borders.
A group of rocky hills almost surround
a large bason, the general receptacle,
the water draining from the vast savanna.
The verdant grasses were soft underfoot
and yielded to golden-brown vested plains.

Envoi
After an hour more,
        like Bartram
having *satisfied my curiosity,*
        in viewing this extraordinary place
and very wonderful work of nature
        I considered other trail stops:
Colclough Hills, Bivens Arm, and Lake Kanapaha.

I had, however, other days ahead
        and decided to heed Coleridge,
who noted:
        Travels is a delicious book
and like all delicious Things,
        you must take but little of it at a time,
and I drove home.

Flight of Savanna Cranes

As we talked, he looked toward the sky.
        They're arriving, he said.
        Who? I asked.
I turned my newcomer's eyes
        to Alachua skies as we stood among
savanna grasses on Payne's Prairie.

The sandhill cranes, he said,
        or savanna cranes,
as Bartram called them.
        The Indians named them Wattoola.
See the flight formation. Listen.
        They alter, gliding and flapping.
A low, loud rattle.

Now, two hundred years after Bartram wrote,
        behold the loud, sonorous, watchful savanna crane
with musical clangor, in detached squadrons
        form the line with wide extended wings,
tip to tip.
        They rise and fall as one bird.

Bartram observed them alighting
        on palms or pines, on lofty roosts.
Naturalists today say this is baffling,
        they do not land in trees.
Did Bartram err or has sandhill behavior changed?
        We watch them and wonder: will they land in trees?

Gopher

A southern gopher is remarkably
different from a northern gopher,
Gopherus polyphemus not Geomys bursarius.

In 1774 Bartram discovered the dens
of the great land tortoise
called Gopher, this strange creature.

An accomplished burrower's
tunnel slopes downward
from its surface, collared
by up-heaved earth.
It runs for twenty feet, and is
gopher-turning-around wide.

The gopher uses
shovel-like front feet,
stubby hind feet,
armed all around with sharp,
flattish strong nails
to dig its tunnel and roundhouse.

Gopher shell, Bartram noted,
is *hard and boney,*
consisting of many regular compartments.
The color is ash or clay.
A camouflage, when motionless,
most would overlook
as a stone or old stump in a field.
Thirty million years without gopher change.

In warm weather gophers emerge daily,
leaving their many guests—
frogs, insects, snakes, perhaps an owl,
to guard their homes.

Bartram noted:
It is astonishing what a weight
one of these creatures will bear;
easily carry any man standing on its back.

I have never tried the experiment.
I wonder if men were smaller
or gophers larger, or both,
in Bartram's time?

Kanapaha Botanical Gardens

I explore Kanapaha Gardens
        on a Sunday morning,
just after sunrise.
        I wander by Bartram's
group of shelly rocks,
        on the banks of a beautiful lake,
partly environed by meadows.

I sniff the fragrant flowers
        of palms and palmettos in patches.
Timucua Indians proclaimed
        the palmetto leaves *Kanapaha.*
I listen to the wind rustle them
        and imagine thatched huts.

Nearby, I skirt Bartram's limestone rocks
        and his *partly encircled spacious sink or grotto,*
which communicates with the lake waters.
I behold
        his large floating field
with golden blossoms waving to and fro.

Zzzz-zz: Zzzz. Zzzp.
        I am bitten, standing by the waters,
because no *brisk cool wind*
kept the persecuting musquitoes
at a distance,
        as it had for Bartram.

Anhinga

I saw at Lake Alice, as Bartram saw
all over Florida,
a very curious bird,
the people call them Snake Birds.

This morning I beheld the progress
of head and neck periscopic,
gliding on the water's surface,
diving, resurfacing, snakelike.

The anhinga then leapt from the water,
to a low, water-overhanging snag
and faced the breeze's currents.
A body shake created rain ripples.

It is blackish green, with large
silver-patched wings.
Its serpent-like neck,
visible when it swims,
gives it the snake bird name.

It has no oil glands
and gets so soaked on a dive
that it cannot fly,
if just out of water,
or in the rain.

As Bartram noted
they delight to sit
on the dry limbs in trees,
hanging over the waters,
with wings and tails expanded.

The anhinga used its dagger-shaped bill
to sense the wind's direction,
moved left a few degrees,
half opened its wings, capturing air currents.

Its snake-like neck actuated,
its serrated bill started
preening from
shoulder to shoulder and down its back.
Anhinga bluish eyes afforded guidance.

The long tail feathers expanded on cue,
and spread wide,
much like a turkey's—
hence another moniker, water-turkey.

Snake bird to some,
and water turkey to others.
I prefer Linnaeus' name A*nhinga anhinga,*
or simply Anhinga.

Franklinia Altamaha

As I gaze out the window …
        I admire my
two-year-old fragile tree,
        Franklinia altamaha.

I have worried at times about
        its survival
since I purchased it from a mail supplier,
        Bartram's Garden stock in Philadelphia,

where William first planted Franklinia
        from his southern collections,
discovered on two or three acres
        near the Altamaha River in Georgia.

It is a flowering tree,
        of the first order for beauty
and fragrance of blossoms:
        the flowers are very large.

During his travels, William collected seeds
        and honored the tree
with Benjamin Franklin's name.

From these seed my tree and others
        are offspring in danger.
Their Altamaha's origins are lost in time,
        but through Quaker gardening
they have survived.

I wonder if my tree will bloom
        with large white fragrant flowers
embellish'd with a large tassel
                or crown of golden stamens?

I wonder if cultivation for two hundred years
will ensure Franklinia's survival
or should we look to genome banks
        and clones?

Reflections on Bartram

William Baldwin,1819

Such, he [Bartram] informed me,
was his partiality
for that delightful country [Florida],
that he often fancied himself
transported thither
in his dreams by night.

John Eatton LeConte, 1854

Mr. Bartram was a man
of unimpeached integrity and veracity,
of primeval simplicity
of manner and honesty,
unsuited to these times,
when such virtues
are not appreciated.

Immeasurably Old and Future Biblical Article

Bartram's *Travels*, published in 1791,
the year of our Constitution,
fifteen years after our Declaration,
parallels these documents.

The Constitution and Declaration speak
of human rights and social conditions.
Bartram writes of nature's being,
natural rights and their importance.

Today, nature's claims and importance
closely relate to human conditions.
Life's web of relationships forms an impalpable,
but real fabric spun tightly.

Bartram's *Travels* is past testimony,
a comparison of present ecological havoc
and a beacon for future conservation.
It is immeasurably old with a biblical future.

≈7≈

ENVOI

There was a child went forth every day,
And the first object he looked upon and
received with wonder or pity or love
Or dread, that object he became,
And that object became part of him for the day
or a certain part of the day . . . .or
for many years or stretching cycles of years.
Seasons pursuing each other. . .

—Walt Whitman

***Leaves of Grass*, 1855**

Applause of Science

Sing applause of science,
        As Walt Whitman did,
In the beauty of poems
        are the tuft and final
applause of science.

Sing science of nature's
        water, rivers, seas
shores, and tides,
        plants, animals, woods,
in sunshine, clouds, rain,
        and storms.
Season, after season…
        Whitman's,
… stretching cycles of years.
        Seasons pursuing each other. . .
O voluptuous coolbreathed earth!

Seasons

With memories of
        Florida's endless season:
lush foliage, idyllic rivers, and rapture skies …

We arrived at our Maryland fourth-floor abode,
        enchanted by panoramic autumn views—
Polychromatic tree canopies
        festoon our balcony's courtyard,
with leaf colors changing from amber to sepia.
        Russet leaves crinkling, aging—
Landscape cues,
        for life changes.

Getting Acquainted

I wander,
        as a naturalist in an alien habitat,
looking, searching for knowns –
        ah, there –
a mockingbird perched in a dogwood!
        Swoosh –
The mockingbird streaks, lands near,
        a large and unfamiliar oak –
white, pin, red, or other?

I amble over,
        photograph the bark and several leaves,
to identify and become oak-acquainted
        for future sauntering's of discovery.

Outside In

Overlooking our balcony,
        bird feeders, and planters,
into the woods—

My study window is an observatory
        for eyes and cameras to follow
nature's changing seasons.

Sightings

Through the window,
I glimpse yellow flybys—
        Warblers?
        Orioles?
        Finches?
No, they are—
yellow maple leaves
in the autumn wind.

Scouts

Feeder seeds, suet, hanging—
        Day 1.
Curious scout arrives,
        quickly perching, taste testing,
flutters away into the woods.
        Day 2.
Other scouts approach,
        land and peck,
take one seed each,
        fly away.
IDs confirmed:
        white-breasted nuthatch and
black-capped chickadee.
        Day 3.
Flock of nuthatches, then
        several chickadees
perch in nearby oaks,
        swoop over
and land on balcony,
        nibble seeds and suet,
surge away.
        Day 4.
Daily visits begin—
        chickadees, nuthatches,
for feeder snacks.
        They soar away
with seeds in their beaks,
        proof of their scouts' discovery.

Autumn's Exit

Tawny leaves,
        like migrating monarchs,
swarm in the autumn winds.
        In morning's sunlight,
barren branches gleam.
        Golden brown leaves litter the ground.
Nature arrays the woods for winter.

Winter Preparation

Sky darkens,
        temperature plummets.
Wind bursts create vortices
        of brown, rust, and yellow leaves.
Gusts become gales.
        Maples are leaf-stripped bare.
Squirrels scamper,
        making nest repairs.

Transition

The morning glory leaves,
        lacing the balcony's railing,
are browning.
        Several flowers are wilted blue.
Glittering hummingbirds and other visitors,
        their bio-alarms sounding,
have flown south.

Hold Outs

As the days shorten,
        three crinkled dry leaves
cling to a knotty branch
        on a naked maple.
The leaves quiver,
        glistening golden
in late autumn's light,
        challenging winter fate:
leaf drop and eco-recycle.

Crows Transformed

Snowflakes twirling—
        Two crows side by side.
Ebony beaks often touch.
        One's raised wing
shelters the other.
        As snowfall continues,
they become snowbirds.

Mockingbird Interlude

1.
A welcoming mockingbird song,
        heard from our balcony.
The glint of the sun on the singer's eye.
2.
On many autumn and winter days,
        you have visited,
Wind-blown, you preened,
        Did you follow me from Florida?
You solitary mockingbird songster!
3.
Festivals of winter arrive.
        Dazzle me with wing bling,
jerk-jerk unbolt your wings.
        Flaunt the white fan patch on each.
Cloak them again in gray feathers.
        Parade and repeat your white flashes.
Expand your tail feathers.
        Flash white semaphores of feasting celebration.
4.
A flight of roving mockers
        invade and forage in grasses and bushes
near your holly tree,
        ready for a raid on remaining berries.
You circle them in a border dance,
        wing flashing and tail fanning,
screaming a territorial warning of
        repeated loud churrs, scratchy chat calls.
You alone, five attackers …

Aroused mockingbird neighbors,
        protecting shared holly berry tree,
band together and charge the intruders
        with dive-bombing tactics,
attack rolls, and strident calls—
        Chew, chewk! Ch'ch'ch'chick,
Chew! Chewk! Chew! –
        And send the raiders into ragged retreat.

5.

In early-morning March frost,
        your beak punctures the wind.
Your body size has tripled,
        the cold wind inflates
your hidden overcoat
        and powder-puffs feathers.
Your wings become a sheltering cape.
        Spring is on the way.

6.

Your continuous, restless lusty song
        from the depths of the holly tree,
sporadic through the April day,
        becomes louder, more frequent—
whistles, trills—into night.

A male invader mockingbird,
        prowling for a mate,
flutters, silently watchful
        from a neighboring magnolia.

From the holly tree,
        your laser-focused warning—
your harsh, dry chew-chewk call—
        And with a nodding glance,
the lone mocker moves on, and
        your love song begins again.

7.
In May, you sing
        a longing tenor aria
from the holly tree.
        A passing female pauses
on a nearby dogwood tree.

In a flash,
        you dive ten feet,
circle loop,
        back to your perch.
Wings flashing, you
        return to your love song.
8.
Later in May,
        he or she?
Twig in beak,
        in holly leaves,
creeping on a branch toward the trunk.
        The start of a nest?
9.
Two in the holly tree,
        in your nest with three
blue-green eggs spotted brown.

Every day,
        you forage, feed and guard
your alert, bright-eyed mate
        with feather-quilted eggs.

Spring Cleaning

White blossoms fleck tips
        of cherry branches.
A foraging squirrel,
        bites off a flowering twig.
scampers up the tree trunk,
        inserts the spring treasure
into a nest of sticks and dry leaves,
        causing winter collectibles—
bits of twigs, snakeskin, and lichens—
        to fly in the late March winds,
spring-cleaning the nest.

The Promise

Pale, mint-green foliage
        with tree bark accents,
flutters as it canopies the courtyard
        against a cerulean sky,
veiled in the humid promise
        of spring showers.

Daffodil green sprouts fill planters,
        later with colors, shades, and hues.
Robins, orioles, and hummingbirds
        will return soon, following
Geese flying in V-formation, now overhead.

Foliage Changes

After autumn's chromatic gamut,
winter's absolutes and dormancy,
and spring's sunshine foliate tints,
now, heavy breathing, transpiring plants.
Summer's swelling leafiness—
shades of green,
an emerald spectrum,
an excited chlorophyll festival.

Awaking

A verdant treescape,
        dark, somber, motionless,
awaits a photographer
        to capture its awakening,
as light tints add
        texture and depth
to foliage arousing at sunrise.

Stormy Evening Ballet

Lightning and thunder
        transformed the woods,
from a darkened stage
        with hidden figures,
into a ballet of nature.

Wind and rain choreographed
        nature's dancing corps.
Maples, ash, oaks, and pines,
        in ageless agile movements,
tilted, rocked backward,
        turned, rose, and outstretched
in a thunderous allegro.

Life Cycle

An autumn tree canopy,
        crinkled leaves tinkling,
like bells—
        memory bells,
        and future bells,
as another life season begins.

ABOUT THE AUTHOR

Thomas Peter Bennett is a Florida native on perpetual sabbatical as an independent scholar and poet. A former professor and natural history museum executive, he is the author of scientific articles and books, as well as poems and collections on topics featured in *The Applause of Science*. After graduating from Florida State University (FSU) with a bachelor's degree in chemistry, Bennett earned his PhD in biochemistry from Rockefeller University and became an assistant professor at Harvard University. He returned to FSU as a professor and chair of biological sciences and later served as special assistant to the president and as acting executive vice president. He began his museum work as the president of the Academy of Natural Sciences of Philadelphia, now of Drexel University. He then became a dean, professor, and the director of the Florida Museum of Natural History at the University of Florida. He became the executive director of the South Florida Museum and retired as emeritus director.

Bennett's poetry pursuits in his youth were linked to the exploration of Florida's woods, swamps, springs, lakes, rivers, beaches, and familiarity with nature. His biophilia was scientifically reinforced through Scouting, high school biology and chemistry studies, and his work as a laboratory assistant at the Southern Bio-Research Laboratory. His scientific interests in nature were reflected in his poetry.

As an undergraduate student at FSU, Bennett assisted chemistry professor Earl Frieden, with whom he published a review article and, later, *Modern Topics in Biochemistry* (1966). His two summers in the undergraduate student program at Jackson Laboratory in Bar Harbor led to *Hike On: Poems from Mount Desert Island, Maine* (2008). Bennett's graduate school mentor, Fritz Lipmann, had encouraged him to "do things not strictly biochemistry." Poetry led him to workshops and studies with the poet Mary Oliver at Bennington College.

His poems have appeared in many publications (see Acknowledgements). The most recent collection is *Florida Sketches: William Baldwin Follows Bartram's Tracks* (2019). Bennett is a member of The Explorers Club and the Cosmos Club.

www.ingramcontent.com/pod-product-compliance
Lightning Source LLC
Chambersburg PA
CBHW020558310726
48979CB00008B/1255/J

* 9 7 8 1 5 9 7 1 3 2 3 3 6 *